Corfu Trave
2024

"Sun-kissed serenity: Navigating the Beaches and Coastal Charms of Corfu"

By

Logan M. William

Introduction

Welcome to Corfu

Nestled in the azure embrace of the Ionian Sea, Corfu unfolds as a timeless jewel within Greece's embrace. Steeped in myth and history, this island effortlessly marries lush landscapes with Venetian elegance, creating an alluring destination for those seeking cultural richness and natural beauty.

The scent of olive groves wafts through the air as you wander through cobbled streets that witness centuries of diverse influences. Corfu Town, a UNESCO World Heritage site, reveals a tapestry of architectural wonders, from the imposing Old and New Fortresses to the charming Liston Promenade.

Beyond its historic charm, Corfu boasts pristine beaches with crystal-clear waters that beckon sun-seekers and water enthusiasts alike. Each corner of the island unfolds a new chapter, from the ancient ruins of Paleokastritsa to the vibrant hues of Kanoni and the enchanting vistas from Mount Pantokrator.

Corfu, a jewel in the Ionian Sea, welcomes travelers with its captivating blend of history, natural beauty, and vibrant culture. This travel guide serves as your gateway to exploring this enchanting Greek island.

In this introduction to Corfu, anticipate a journey through time and nature. This sojourn intertwines Greek mythology with Venetian grace, creating an experience that resonates with the island's timeless allure. Welcome to Corfu, where history, culture, and nature converge in harmonious beauty.

Chapter One
Overview of Corfu

Nestled off the western coast of Greece, Corfu boasts lush landscapes, crystal-clear waters, and a rich tapestry of historical influences. Every corner tells a story of its diverse past, from ancient ruins to Venetian architecture.

Delve into Corfu's intriguing history, marked by Venetian, French, and British influences. Uncover the island's cultural tapestry through its festivals, traditions, and warm hospitality. As you embark on your Corfu adventure, let this guide be your companion to unlocking the secrets of this Mediterranean gem.

Natural Beauty

Blessed with lush greenery, Corfu's landscape is a symphony of olive groves, cypress trees, and vibrant wildflowers.

The island's diverse terrain ranges from golden beaches lapped by turquoise waters to rugged mountains offering panoramic views.

Historical Significance

Corfu's history is a mosaic shaped by ancient civilizations, including the Greeks, Romans, Byzantines, Venetians, and British. Explore remnants of the past through archaeological sites, fortresses, and charming villages that echo tales of centuries gone by.

Architectural Marvels

Corfu Town, a UNESCO World Heritage Site, showcases a blend of Venetian, French, and British architecture. The Liston Promenade, the Old and New Fortresses, and the Spianada Square are testaments to the island's rich historical and cultural heritage.

Mediterranean Flavors

The island's cuisine mirrors its diverse influences, offering a delectable fusion of Greek,

Italian, and British flavors. Indulge in local specialties such as moussaka, pastitsada, and sofrito while savoring the famed Corfiot olive oil.

Warm Hospitality

Beyond its physical beauty, Corfu is renowned for its warm and welcoming locals. Embrace the laid-back lifestyle, engage in friendly conversations, and immerse yourself in the island's unique community.

Corfu's allure is its ability to seamlessly weave together nature, history, and culture, creating an unforgettable destination for those seeking a harmonious Mediterranean escape.

Historical Tapestry

Corfu's rich history unfolds like the pages of a captivating epic shaped by the footsteps of ancient civilizations. From its origins as a Greek colony in the 8th century BCE to subsequent Roman, Byzantine, and Venetian rule, the island has witnessed the ebb and flow of diverse influences.

Key Historical Periods

1. Ancient Greek Roots: Established by the Corinthians in the 8th century BCE, Corfu thrived as a vital Greek colony, contributing to maritime trade and cultural exchange.

2. Roman and Byzantine Era: The island transitioned to Roman rule in 229 BCE and later became part of the Byzantine Empire. During this period, Corfu's strategic location was crucial in regional politics.

3. Venetian Dominion: The Venetians left an indelible mark on Corfu, fortifying the island with impressive structures such as the Old and New Fortresses. This era of Venetian influence lasted for four centuries.

4. French and British Interludes: Brief periods of French and British occupation followed the fall of the Venetian Republic. Each foreign rule left its imprint on the island's architecture and governance.

5. Union with Greece: Corfu became part of modern Greece in 1864, solidifying its connection with the Hellenic world. The island's historical layers are visible in its archaeological sites, museums, and cultural traditions.

Cultural Kaleidoscope

1. Festivals and Celebrations: Corfu's calendar is adorned with vibrant festivals, including the grand Easter celebration with the throwing of ceramic pots and the Corfu Summer Festival, featuring cultural events and performances.

2. Local Traditions: The island's cultural fabric is woven with unique traditions, such as the

Corfiot wedding custom of throwing rice and the renowned Corfu Philharmonic Society, symbolizing the island's love for music.

3. Arts and Crafts: Corfu's artisans are committed to preserving and passing down age-old craftsmanship, From traditional ceramics to intricate embroidery. Explore local markets to witness the legacy of these artistic endeavors.

In essence, Corfu's history and culture create a captivating mosaic, inviting visitors to explore the layers of its past while savoring the vibrant tapestry of its present-day traditions.

Chapter Two

Getting There

Embarking on your Corfu adventure involves navigating various transportation options and considering essential travel tips to ensure a smooth journey.

Transportation Options

1. By Air: Corfu International Airport, "Ioannis Kapodistrias" (CFU) is the main gateway. Direct flights connect Corfu to major European cities during the tourist season. Upon arrival, taxis and buses provide convenient transfers to different island parts.

2. By Sea: Ferries and cruise ships offer an alternative scenic route to Corfu. The island's ports, including the main one in Corfu Town (Kerkyra), welcome ferry connections from Igoumenitsa and other Ionian Islands.

Travel Tips

1. Peak Season Preparations: If visiting during the high tourist season (summer), booking flights and accommodations well in advance is advisable. The island experiences an influx of visitors seeking sun, sea, and cultural exploration.

2. Off-Peak Advantages: Consider traveling during the shoulder seasons (spring and fall) for a more relaxed experience. You'll still enjoy pleasant weather, and attractions may be less crowded.

3. Local Transportation: Once on the island, various transportation options await. Renting a car allows you to explore Corfu's diverse landscapes independently. Alternatively, public buses and taxis provide convenient ways to navigate the island.

4. Navigating Corfu Town: The historic center of Corfu Town is best explored on foot. Its narrow streets and alleys reveal charming corners, historic landmarks, and enticing local shops.

5. Currency and Payments: The official currency is the Euro (€). While major establishments accept credit cards, carrying some cash for smaller businesses and local markets is advisable.

6. Language: Greek is the official language, but English is widely spoken in tourist areas. Learning a few basic Greek phrases can enhance your experience and show appreciation for the local culture.

By considering these travel tips and choosing the transportation mode that suits your preferences, you'll set the stage for a seamless journey to discover the wonders of Corfu. Safe travels!

Chapter Three

Exploring Corfu Town

Corfu Town, known as Kerkyra, is a living testament to the island's rich history, boasting a captivating blend of Venetian, French, and British influences. Immerse yourself in the following facets of this charming town:

1. Historical Landmarks

Liston Promenade: A picturesque esplanade adorned with arched colonnades, Liston is a hub of cafes, restaurants, and vibrant street life. It's an ideal spot for strolls and people-watching.

Old Fortress (Palaio Frourio): Dating back to the Byzantine era, this fortress offers panoramic views of the town and the sea. Explore its labyrinthine passages and visit the Church of St. George.

New Fortress (Neo Frourio): Built by the Venetians, the New Fortress provides a glimpse into Corfu's military history. Climb to the top for breathtaking vistas of the surrounding landscapes.

Achilleion Palace: Located just outside Corfu Town, this palace, built by Empress of Austria Elisabeth of Bavaria (Sisi), offers a majestic retreat with stunning gardens and imperial architecture.

2. Charming Streets and Venetian Architecture

Corfu Old Town: Wander through the labyrinthine streets of the UNESCO-listed Old Town, a maze of narrow alleys lined with pastel-colored buildings, artisan shops, and hidden squares.

Spianada Square: One of the largest squares in Greece, Spianada is surrounded by elegant buildings and features the Maitland Rotunda. It's a central meeting point and hosts cultural events.

Kantounia: Explore the "Kantounia," the charming alleys that cross the old town. Each corner reveals architectural gems, small churches, and glimpscs of local life.

3. Cultural Experiences

  The Corfu Museum of Asian Art, located in the St. Michael and St. George Palace, features exhibits from an impressive collection of Asian art, reflecting the island's historical connections.

Corfu Archaeological Museum: Delve into the island's past through artifacts and exhibits, providing insight into Corfu's diverse cultural influences.

Churches and Monasteries: Corfu Town is home to numerous churches and monasteries, each with its unique history and architectural style. The Church of Saint Spyridon, the island's patron saint, is a significant pilgrimage site.

Corfu Town's allure lies not only in its historical landmarks but also in the vibrant atmosphere of its streets, the warmth of its people, and the seamless fusion of different cultural legacies.

Exploring Corfu Town is a journey through time and a celebration of the island's enduring charm.

Chapter Four

Beach Escapes in Corfu

Corfu's coastline is a paradise for beach enthusiasts, offering diverse sandy shores, crystal-clear waters, and scenic landscapes. Here are some of the top beach escapes on the island.

1. Paleokastritsa Beach

Location: Nestled on the western coast, Paleokastritsa boasts azure waters and lush green surroundings.

Highlights: Explore the nearby Monastery of Paleokastritsa perched on a hill, providing panoramic coastline views.

2. Glyfada Beach

Location: Situated on the western side of Corfu, Glyfada is renowned for its golden sand and clear waters..

Activities: Water sports enthusiasts can indulge in activities like jet-skiing, while others can relax at beachfront tavernas.

3. Sidari Beach

Location: Located on the northern coast, Sidari is famous for its unique sandstone formations, the Canal d'Amour.

Legend: According to local lore, couples who swim through the Canal d'Amour will get married soon.

4. Agios Gordios Beach

is located on the western side; cliffs and olive groves surround Agios Gordios.

Sunset Views: The beach offers spectacular sunset views, creating a romantic ambiance for evening strolls.

5. Issos Beach

Location: Situated on the southwest coast, Issos is known for its long sandy beaches and dunes.

Windsurfing Haven: The consistent winds make Issos popular for windsurfing and other water sports.

6. Kontogialos Beach (Pelekas Beach)

Location: Curving along the western coastline, Kontogialos is surrounded by hills and offers panoramic views.

Traditional Village: Nearby Pelekas village provides a taste of conventional Corfiot life and a vantage point for breathtaking sunsets.

7. Kavos Beach

Location: Situated on the southern tip, Kavos is famous for its lively atmosphere and nightlife.

Party Scene: The beach has vibrant bars and clubs, making it a hotspot for those seeking a lively social scene.

8. Myrtiotissa Beach

Location: Tucked away on the western coast, Myrtiotissa is often regarded as one of the most beautiful and secluded beaches.

Natural Setting: Surrounded by cliffs and greenery, this beach offers a tranquil escape and is popular among nudists.

Whether you seek vibrant beachfront activities or secluded natural beauty, Corfu's beaches cater to various preferences, promising a rejuvenating and sun-soaked experience by the Ionian Sea.

Top Beaches to Relax and Unwind in Corfu

Corfu's serene beaches offer idyllic settings for those seeking tranquility and relaxation. Here are some top beaches where you can unwind amidst natural beauty.

1. Glyfada Beach

Ambiance: With its soft golden sand and clear waters, Glyfada is a haven for relaxation.

Facilities: Sunbeds and umbrellas are available, and beachfront tavernas offer a laid-back atmosphere.

2. Agios Gordios Beach

Surroundings: Nestled between cliffs, Agios Gordios provides a peaceful escape.

Scenic Views: Enjoy the stunning sunset views over the Ionian Sea, creating a magical atmosphere.

3. Kontogialos Beach (Pelekas Beach)

Panoramic Setting: Surrounded by hills, Kontogialos offers a tranquil environment for unwinding.

Local Charm: Nearby Pelekas village adds to the authentic and relaxed atmosphere.

4. Myrtiotissa Beach

Secluded Paradise: Often considered one of Corfu's most beautiful beaches, Myrtiotissa is secluded and surrounded by greenery.

Natural Setting: Embrace the natural beauty, and take in the serene ambiance away from the bustling crowds.

5. Rovinia Beach

Hidden Gem: Accessible by a scenic walking trail, Rovinia is a quieter beach with pebble shores.

Nature Retreat: The surrounding cliffs and lush vegetation create a secluded and peaceful environment.

6. Santa Barbara Beach

Pristine Waters: Located on the southeast coast, Santa Barbara Beach boasts crystal-clear waters and a relaxed atmosphere.

Water Activities: While calm most of the day, the afternoon breeze suits it for windsurfing and other water activities.

7. Halikounas Beach

Natural Beauty: Halikounas is a long, sandy beach surrounded by dunes and the Korission Lagoon.

Birdwatching: Nature enthusiasts can explore the nearby lagoon, home to various bird species.

8. Almyros Beach

Peaceful Retreat: Situated on the north coast, Almyros Beach offers a serene escape from the busier tourist areas.

Family-Friendly: The shallow waters suit families, and the quiet surroundings enhance relaxation.

As you explore these tranquil beaches, each with its unique charm, you'll discover the perfect spots to unwind, bask in the sun, and savor the calming rhythm of the Ionian Sea.

Chapter Five
Culinary Delights in Corfu

Corfu's culinary scene is a flavorful journey through the island's rich history and cultural influences. Indulge in a variety of dishes that showcase the unique blend of Greek, Italian, and British flavors:

1. Moussaka

Description: A classic Greek dish, moussaka features layers of eggplant, minced meat (often lamb or beef), and béchamel sauce, baked to perfection.

Local Twist: Corfu's moussaka may include local ingredients, adding a unique touch to this beloved dish.

2. Pastitsada

Description: Pastitsada is a hearty Corfiot stew typically made with beef or rooster, cooked in a rich tomato and wine sauce with a medley of spices.

Serving Style: It's often served over pasta or mashed potatoes, creating a comforting and flavorful meal.

3. Sofrito

Description: A Corfiot specialty, sofrito features thinly sliced beef cooked in white wine and garlic sauce, resulting in tender and aromatic meat.

Accompaniment: It's commonly served with mashed potatoes or rice.

4. Bourdeto

Description: Bourdeto is a spicy fish stew with local catches, such as scorpionfish or rockfish, simmered in a tomato and chili sauce.

Serving Style: Enjoy bordello with crusty bread to soak up the flavorful broth.

5. Corfiot Olive Oil

Quality: Corfu is renowned for its high-quality olive oil, a staple in its cuisine. Drizzle it over salads, use it as a dip, or enhance the flavors of various dishes.

6. Kumquat Products

Specialty: Corfu's unique kumquat fruit is celebrated in various forms, including kumquat liqueur, marmalade, and sweets. Explore local markets for these delightful treats.

7. Local Cheeses

Varieties: Taste the local cheeses such as graviera, feta, and ladotyri. These cheeses are often featured in salads, pies, or standalone appetizers.

8. Sweets - Pastries and Desserts

Favorites: Indulge in traditional sweets like baklava, galaktoboureko (custard-filled pastry), and mandolato (nougat with almonds).

9. Local Wines

Varieties: Corfu produces excellent wines, both red and white. Pair your meals with a glass of local wine to enhance the dining experience.

10. Taverna Culture

Experience: Embrace the taverna culture, where dining is not just about the food but also the lively atmosphere, traditional music, and warm hospitality.

Corfu's culinary delights offer a delightful fusion of flavors, showcasing the island's unique history and cultural influences. From savory stews to sweet treats, every bite celebrates Corfiot gastronomy.

Recommended Restaurants and Cafes in Corfu

Corfu's dining scene offers diverse establishments, from traditional tavernas to charming cafes, where you can savor the island's rich culinary heritage. Here are some recommended venues to enhance your gastronomic experience:

1. Taverna Tripa

Location: Corfu Town

Highlights: Known for its authentic Corfiot cuisine, Taverna Tripa offers a cozy atmosphere and traditional dishes, including pastitsada and sofrito.

2. Salto Wine Bar & Bistro

Location: Corfu Town

Highlights: A wine lover's haven, Salto Wine Bar & Bistro pairs excellent local wines with a Corfiot and Mediterranean flavors menu.

3. Etrusco Restaurant

Location: Corfu Town

Highlights: Etrusco combines Italian and Greek influences, offering a menu with various pasta dishes, seafood, and local specialties.

4. Rex Restaurant-Corfu Town

Location: Corfu Town

Highlights: With a prime location on the Liston Promenade, Rex Restaurant-Corfu Town serves classic Greek dishes in an elegant setting.

5. Oino Mageiremata

Location: Corfu Town

Highlights: This charming restaurant uses fresh, local ingredients to create a menu that reflects Corfu's culinary traditions.

6. La Cucina Di Nonna

Location: Corfu Town

Highlights: A family-run restaurant, La Cucina Di Nonna specializes in homemade Italian and Corfiot dishes, offering a warm and welcoming atmosphere.

7. To Perasma

Location: Paleokastritsa

Highlights: Nestled in the picturesque Paleokastritsa, To Perasma boasts stunning sea views and serves fresh seafood and traditional Greek cuisine.

8. Bella Ellada

Location: Gouvia

Highlights: Overlooking the marina, Bella Ellada offers a menu of Greek and Mediterranean flavors, showcasing locally sourced ingredients.

9. Avli Restaurant

Location: Nissaki

Highlights: Avli Restaurant, set in a beautiful garden, provides a romantic setting in which to enjoy seafood and Greek specialties.

10. Klimataria

Location: Corfu Town

Highlights: Tucked in a historic building, Klimataria is known for its traditional Greek dishes and warm hospitality.

Cafes

1. Art Café:

Location: Corfu Town

Highlights: A cozy spot for coffee lovers, Art Café offers a selection of artisanal coffees and pastries in a relaxed setting.

2. Café Liston

Location: Corfu Town

Highlights: Situated on the Liston Promenade, Café Liston is perfect for people-watching while enjoying coffee, desserts, and a view of the cricket pitch.

3. Koukoutsis Café

Location: Paleokastritsa

Highlights: Overlooking the sea, Koukoutsis Café is a charming spot to relax with a coffee or indulge in homemade desserts.

4. La Ponta

Location: Kanoni

Highlights: With panoramic views of Mouse Island, La Ponta offers a tranquil atmosphere in which to enjoy coffee, refreshments, and light bites.

5. Pralina Experience

Location: Corfu Town

Highlights: The Pralina Experience is a sweet haven, offering a tempting array of chocolates, pastries, and artisanal desserts.

These recommended restaurants and cafes provide a delightful blend of flavors, ambiance, and hospitality, inviting you to savor the best of Corfu's culinary offerings.

Chapter six
Outdoor Adventures in Corfu

Corfu's diverse landscapes provide a playground for outdoor enthusiasts, from pristine beaches to lush mountains. Corfu has something to offer whether you seek adrenaline-pumping activities or leisurely nature exploration. Consider the following outdoor adventures:

1. Hiking Trails

Corfu Trail: Embark on the Corfu Trail, a long-distance hiking path that spans the entire island. Traverse through olive groves, charming villages, and scenic landscapes, enjoying panoramic views.

2. Water Activities

Windsurfing and Kitesurfing: The island's consistent winds make spots like Agios Georgios and Issos Beach ideal for windsurfing and kitesurfing. Rental centers provide equipment and lessons.

Snorkeling and Diving: Explore Corfu's underwater world by snorkeling or diving. Crystal-clear waters reveal vibrant marine life and underwater caves, with dive sites near Paleokastritsa and Kassiopi.

3. Mountain Biking

Exploring Villages: Rent a mountain bike and explore the scenic villages and off-road trails. The hilly terrain offers both challenging routes and leisurely rides through olive groves.

4. Boat Tours and Kayaking

Sea Caves Exploration: Join boat tours or rent a kayak to explore the sea caves and hidden coves along the coastline. Paleokastritsa and Kassiopi are popular starting points.

5. Quad Biking

Off-Road Excursions: Navigate Corfu's diverse landscapes on a quad bike. Guided tours take you off the beaten path, through olive groves, and to panoramic viewpoints.

6. Horseback Riding

Trail Rides: Experience the island from a different perspective with horseback riding excursions. Trails meander through olive groves, along beaches, and into the Countryside.

7. Golfing

Corfu Golf Club: Tee off at the Corfu Golf Club in the Ropa Valley. The 18-hole course offers stunning views of the surrounding hills and the Ionian Sea.

8. Jeep Safaris

Off-Road Exploration: Join a Jeep safari to discover Corfu's hidden gems. Traverse rugged terrains, visit traditional villages, and enjoy breathtaking views from elevated vantage points.

9. Paragliding

Bird's Eye View: Soar above Corfu's landscapes with paragliding experiences. Take off from the hillsides and enjoy a bird's eye view of the coastline and Countryside.

10. Caving

Exploring Underground: Corfu has several caves waiting to be explored. Aqualand Cave, near Paleokastritsa, is known for its stalactite formations and underground pools.

Whether you're an adrenaline junkie or seeking a more relaxed outdoor experience, Corfu's natural beauty and diverse terrain provide the perfect backdrop for a variety of outdoor adventures.

Hiking Trails in Corfu

Corfu's diverse landscapes, ranging from mountainous terrain to coastal paths, offer many hiking opportunities for nature enthusiasts. Lace up your hiking boots and explore the island's scenic trails:

1. Corfu Trail

Distance: Approximately 220 kilometers (137 miles)

Description: The Corfu Trail is a long-distance hiking route spanning the island. Divided into ten sections, it takes you through olive groves, picturesque villages, and rugged landscapes. Highlights include Angelokastro, Lakones, and the stunning vistas of the Pantokrator mountain.

2. Angelokastro Trail

Distance: Approximately 7 kilometers (4.3 miles)

Description: This circular trail leads to Angelokastro, a medieval fortress perched atop a cliff. The route provides panoramic views of the Ionian Sea and explores the surrounding Countryside.

3. Pantokrator Summit Trail

Distance: Approximately 5 kilometers (3.1 miles)

Description: Ascend to the summit of Mount Pantokrator, Corfu's highest peak. The trail offers a challenging yet rewarding hike, and the panoramic views from the top are unparalleled.

4. Kaiser's Throne Trail

Distance: Approximately 4 kilometers (2.5 miles)

Description: Starting from Pelekas village, this trail leads to Kaiser's Throne, a viewpoint offering breathtaking vistas of the western coastline and the Ionian Sea.

5. Paleokastritsa Monastery Trail

Distance: Approximately 2.5 kilometers (1.5 miles)

Description: Explore the scenic trails around Paleokastritsa Monastery, weaving through cypress and olive groves. The monastery itself provides a serene setting overlooking the sea.

6. Lakones to Paleokastritsa Beach Trail

Distance: Approximately 2.5 kilometers (1.5 miles)

Description: This coastal trail connects the village of Lakones to Paleokastritsa Beach. Revel in panoramic views of the rugged coastline and turquoise waters.

7. Ermones to Glyfada Trail

Distance: Approximately 7 kilometers (4.3 miles)

Description: Starting at Ermones Bay, this trail takes you through lush vegetation and offers stunning views as you descend towards the sandy shores of Glyfada Beach.

8. Agios Georgios to Arkoudeas Trail

Distance: Approximately 12 kilometers (7.5 miles)

Description: This trail along the southwestern coast takes you from Agios Georgios village to Arkoudilas Beach. Experience diverse landscapes, including sandy stretches and rocky outcrops.

9.Kavos to Lefkimmi Trail

Distance: Approximately 12 kilometers (7.5 miles)

Description: Explore the southern tip of Corfu by hiking from Kavos to Lefkimmi. This trail offers a mix of coastal scenery, dunes, and traditional villages.

10. Arkoudilas Beach to Marathias Trail

Distance: Approximately 5 kilometers (3.1 miles)

Description: Traverse the scenic route from Arkoudilas Beach to Marathias village, enjoying views of the Ionian Sea and the lush Corfiot countryside.

Before embarking on any hike, ensure you are well-prepared with appropriate gear, sufficient water, and knowledge of the trail conditions. Whether seeking panoramic mountain vistas or coastal adventures, Corfu's hiking trails promise a journey through nature's wonders.

Water Activities in Corfu

Corfu's crystal-clear waters and diverse coastline provide the perfect playground for various water activities. Whether you seek exhilarating adventures or serene exploration, the Ionian Sea invites you to dive into a world of aquatic experiences:

1. Windsurfing and Kitesurfing

Popular Spots: Agios Georgios, Issos Beach, and Almiros Beach

Description: The island's consistent winds make it an ideal destination for windsurfing and kitesurfing. Rental centers offer equipment and lessons for all skill levels.

2. Snorkeling and Diving

Notable Sites: Paleokastritsa, Kassiopi, and Ermones

Description: Explore Corfu's vibrant underwater world through snorkeling or diving. Discover colorful marine life, underwater caves, and captivating seascapes.

3. Boat Tours and Kayaking

Sea Caves Exploration: Join boat tours to explore the sea caves along the coastline, particularly near Paleokastritsa and Kassiopi. Alternatively, rent a kayak for a more personal adventure.

4. Sailing and Yachting

Marinas: Gouvia Marina, Corfu Town Marina

Description: Set sail around the Ionian Islands or charter a yacht for a luxurious experience. Corfu's marinas cater to sailing enthusiasts, providing a gateway to explore the stunning archipelago.

5. Jet Skiing

Popular Spots: Various beaches, including Glyfada and Ipsos

Description: Experience the thrill of jet skiing along Corfu's coastline. Rental services are available at several beaches, offering an adrenaline-pumping aquatic adventure.

6. Parasailing:

Locations: Gouvia, Ipsos, and Glyfada

Description: Soar above the sea with parasailing adventures. Enjoy breathtaking views of the coastline while being towed by a boat, creating an unforgettable experience.

7. Paddleboarding

Scenic Spots: Corfu's calm bays and beaches

Description: Try paddleboarding in the tranquil waters around Corfu. It's a relaxing way to explore the coastline and enjoy the scenic beauty at your own pace.

8. Water Skiing

Locations: Gouvia, Ipsos, and Glyfada

Description: Glide across the water with water skiing sessions at various beaches. Whether you're a beginner or an experienced skier, Corfu offers suitable spots.

9. Cruises and Island Hopping

Options: Day cruises and island-hopping excursions

Description: Join a cruise to explore nearby islands or take a day trip to Paxos and Antipaxos. Discover hidden coves, swim in secluded bays, and enjoy the charm of neighboring isles.

10. Fishing Trips

Organized Tours: Available in various coastal towns

Description: Enjoy a relaxing fishing trip to experience the traditional activity and possibly catch your dinner. Many local operators offer guided fishing excursions.

Corfu's waters provide a dynamic canvas for water activities, catering to thrill-seekers and those seeking a more relaxed aquatic experience. Dive into the Ionian Sea and embrace the myriad opportunities for exploration and enjoyment.

.

Chapter seven
Hidden Gems in Corfu

Beyond the well-trodden paths and popular attractions, Corfu harbors hidden gems that unveil the island's authentic charm and lesser-known wonders. Discover these enchanting spots off the beaten track:

1. Bella Vista in Lakones

Location: Lakones Village

Highlights: Perched on a hill, Bella Vista offers a panoramic view of Paleokastritsa and the Ionian Sea. Enjoy the breathtaking sunset from this charming vantage point.

2. Agios Nikolaos Church

Location: Porto Timoni, Afionas

Highlights: Nestled on a hill overlooking the double bay of Porto Timoni, this church provides a serene retreat and stunning coastline views.

3. Korission Lake

Location: Southwest Corfu

Highlights: A tranquil natural reserve, Korission Lake is surrounded by dunes and is a haven for birdwatching. Take a peaceful stroll along the shore.

4. Kouloura Village

Location: Northeast Corfu

Highlights: A picturesque fishing village with a small harbor, Kouloura exudes traditional charm. Enjoy a leisurely meal at a waterfront taverna and savor the tranquility.

5. Porto Timoni Beach

Location: Afionas

Highlights: Accessible via a scenic hike, Porto Timoni is a hidden gem with two sandy beaches separated by a narrow strip of land. The view from the hilltop is truly captivating.

6. Perithia Village

Location: North Corfu

Highlights: Explore the deserted village of Perithia, a time capsule of Venetian architecture. The town offers a glimpse into Corfu's past and features traditional tavernas.

7. Agios Gordios Viewpoint

Location: Agios Gordios

Highlights: Venture up the hill behind Agios Gordios for a stunning panoramic view of the beach and the lush coastline. It's a peaceful spot away from the crowds.

8. Arkoudilas Beach and Lighthouse

Location: Southern Corfu

Highlights: A secluded beach with golden sands, Arkoudilas is complemented by a historic lighthouse. It's an off-the-beaten-path destination offering tranquility.

9. Vlacherna Monastery

Location: Kanoni

Highlights: Connected to the mainland by a causeway, Vlacherna Monastery is a serene retreat with views of Pontikonisi (Mouse Island) and the distant mountains.

10. Benitses Roman Baths

Location: Benitses

Highlights: Uncover the remains of ancient Roman Baths in the coastal village of Benitses.

These historical ruins provide a glimpse into Corfu's past.

11. Achilleion Gardens at Dafni

Location: Dafni Village

Highlights: Explore the lush gardens surrounding the Achilleion Palace. The gardens offer tranquility and breathtaking views of the Ionian Sea.

Discovering Corfu's hidden gems allows you to connect with the island's authentic character and witness its lesser-explored beauty. Venture off the tourist trail and embrace the serenity and uniqueness of these enchanting places.

Off-the-Beaten-Path Discoveries in Corfu

For those who seek the road less traveled, Corfu unveils hidden treasures away from the tourist hubs. Embark on a journey of discovery and explore these off-the-beaten-path gems:

1. Agios Spyridon Church

Location: Old Perithia Village

Highlights: Nestled in the abandoned village of Old Perithia, Agios Spyridon Church is a testament to the island's history. Wander through the deserted stone streets and savor the tranquility.

2. Ropa Valley Olive Grove

Location: Ropa Valley

Highlights: Roam through the expansive olive groves of Ropa Valley, where centuries-old trees whisper stories of Corfu's agricultural heritage.

The tranquility of this rural landscape offers a peaceful retreat.

3. Kato Garouna Village

Location: Central Corfu

Highlights: Tucked away in the island's interior, Kato Garouna exudes traditional charm. Wander its narrow lanes, adorned with colorful flowers, and encounter the warmth of local hospitality.

4. Paramonas Beach

Location: Southwest Corfu

Highlights: Escape the crowds at Paramonas Beach, a tranquil stretch of pebbly shore surrounded by olive groves. Revel in the simplicity and natural beauty of this lesser-known coastal haven.

5.Kato Pavliana Village

Location: Northwest Corfu

Highlights: Immerse yourself in the authentic atmosphere of Kato Pavliana, a traditional village where time seems to stand still. The town offers a glimpse into Corfu's rural life.

6. Kanouli Beach

Location: South Corfu

Highlights: A hidden gem, Kanouli Beach boasts golden sands and emerald waters. Its secluded nature provides a serene environment for those seeking a quiet escape.

7. Mon Repos Estate

Location: Kanoni

Highlights: Explore the historic Mon Repos Estate, once the summer residence of the Greek royal family. Wander through the lush gardens and discover the neoclassical architecture of the villa.

8.Agios Georgios Pagon

Location: Northwest Corfu

Highlights: While Agios Georgios Pagon is not entirely undiscovered, its western stretch is often less frequented. Savor the tranquil setting and breathtaking sunset vistas.

9. Arkadades Village

Location: Northwest Corfu

Highlights: Experience the tranquility of Arkadades, a village surrounded by olive groves and rolling hills. Stroll through its narrow lanes and savor the authentic Greek ambiance.

10. Chlomos Village

Location: Southeast Corfu

Highlights: Perched on a hilltop, Chlomos offers panoramic views of the Ionian Sea. Its narrow alleys, traditional architecture, and local tavernas contribute to its charming appeal.

11. Peroulades Village

Location: Northwest Corfu

Highlights: Venture to Peroulades, where you'll discover the unique Sunset Beach (Logas Beach). Enjoy a breathtaking sunset from the cliffs overlooking the azure waters.

Discovering Corfu's off-the-beaten-path wonders unveils a side of the island that goes beyond the typical tourist experience. Embrace the serenity and authenticity of these hidden gems, where each discovery adds a layer to the island's rich tapestry.

Local Secrets in Corfu

Unlock the hidden treasures and insider tips cherished by Corfu's residents. Dive into the local secrets that add an authentic touch to your island experience:

1. Rex: The Café of Locals

Location: Corfu Town

Secret Tip: Join the locals at Café Rex on the Liston Promenade. Sip on a Greek coffee or ouzo and absorb the laid-back atmosphere while enjoying views of the cricket pitch.

2. Mirtiotissa Beach - The Hippie Hideaway

Location: West Corfu

Secret Tip: Mirtiotissa Beach, often called the **"Hippie Beach,"** is a local favorite. Embrace the bohemian vibe, pristine sands, and clear waters for a more secluded coastal experience.

3. Hidden Tavernas in Pelekas

Location: Pelekas Village

Secret Tip: Wander the streets of Pelekas and discover hidden tavernas favored by locals. These gems serve traditional Corfiot dishes with a personal touch.

4. St. Spyridon Church Night Walk

Location: Corfu Town

Secret Tip: Experience the magic of St. Spyridon Church at night. The soft glow of the church against the dark sky creates a captivating ambiance. It's a serene and lesser-known moment.

5. Lakones Village Balcony

Location: Lakones Village

Secret Tip: Head to Lakones and find the charming balcony overlooking the Ionian Sea. It's a perfect spot to enjoy a quiet moment and savor the stunning sunset.

6. Secret Viewpoint in Pelekas

Location: Pelekas Village

Secret Tip: Ascend to a hidden viewpoint in Pelekas for a breathtaking panorama. Capture the sunset or enjoy the tranquility away from the bustling crowds.

7. Kato Korakiana Traditional Shops

Location: Kato Korakiana

Secret Tip: Explore the traditional shops in Kato Korakiana. From local crafts to homemade products, these shops offer a glimpse into Corfu's artisanal heritage.

8. Kommeno Peninsula Retreat

Location: Kommeno Peninsula

Secret Tip: Seek out the quiet retreats on the Kommeno Peninsula. Hidden spots along the coastline offer peace and seclusion, perfect for a tranquil escape.

9. Local Wine Tasting in Doukades:

Location: Doukades Village

Secret Tip: Visit the local wineries in Doukades for a personalized wine-tasting experience. Sample exquisite wines and learn about the island's viticulture.

10. Agios Mattheos Village Square

Location: Agios Mattheos

Secret Tip: Spend an evening in the village square of Agios Mattheos. Join the locals at a traditional kafeneio, enjoy a Greek coffee, and immerse yourself in the authentic atmosphere.

11. Nymphes Waterfall Hideaway

Location: Nymphes Village

Secret Tip: Venture to Nymphes to discover a hidden waterfall. This serene spot, surrounded by lush greenery, offers a refreshing escape from the summer heat.

Exploring these local secrets unveils a deeper, more intimate Corfu. Embrace the recommendations residents cherish, and you'll discover a side of the island that goes beyond the guidebooks.

Chapter Eight

Practical Information for Your Corfu Adventure

Before embarking on your journey to Corfu, equip yourself with practical information to ensure a smooth and enjoyable experience:

1. Travel Documents

Make sure your passport is up to date with at least six months remaining before your trip.

Verify the necessary visas depending on your country.

2. Currency

The official currency is the Euro (€). ATMs are widely available in towns, and credit cards are accepted in most establishments.

3. Weather

Corfu enjoys a Mediterranean climate with warm summers and mild winters. In order to pack appropriately, check the weather prediction for the dates of your trip.

4. Language

The official language is Greek. English is widely spoken in tourist areas, but learning basic Greek phrases can enhance your experience.

5. Transportation

Airport: Corfu International Airport (CFU) serves the island, offering domestic and international flights.

Public Transport: Buses connect major towns, while taxis and car rentals provide flexible transportation.

Ferries: Explore neighboring islands or the mainland via ferries departing from Corfu's port.

6. Accommodation

Corfu offers a range of accommodation options, including hotels, resorts, villas, and guesthouses. Plan ahead, particularly during the busiest travel times.

7. Health and Safety

Carry any necessary prescription medications and have travel insurance that covers medical emergencies.

Corfu has medical facilities, and the European Health Insurance Card (EHIC) may provide coverage for EU citizens.

8. Local Etiquette

Greece is renowned for its friendly hospitality. Greet with a friendly "Kalimera" (Good morning) and embrace the relaxed pace of life.

When visiting churches or monasteries, wear modest clothing.

9. Time Zone

Corfu operates on Eastern European Time (EET), which is UTC+2 during standard time and UTC+3 during daylight saving time.

10. Electricity

50 Hz is the frequency, and 230 V is the standard voltage. Type C and Type F electrical outlets are used. Bring a travel adapter if needed.

11. Cuisine and Tipping

Sample local dishes like moussaka, pastitsada, and seafood specialties. Tipping is customary, usually rounding up the bill or leaving 5-10% in restaurants.

12. Shopping Hours

Most shops follow a siesta schedule, closing for a few hours in the afternoon. Larger towns may have more extended hours.

13. Emergency Numbers

In emergencies, dial 112 for general assistance, 100 for police, 166 for medical emergencies, and 199 for the fire department.

14. Wi-Fi and Connectivity

-Numerous cafes, hotels, and public areas have Wi-Fi. Consider getting a local SIM card for mobile data during your stay.

15. Cultural Events

Check for local festivals, celebrations, and cultural events during your visit. These experiences offer insight into Corfu's traditions.

Arming yourself with these practical details will contribute to a seamless and delightful exploration of Corfu. Now, immerse yourself in the island's beauty, history, and warm hospitality. Safe travels!

Currency in Corfu

The official currency of Corfu, as well as the entire country of Greece, is the Euro (€). Here are some essential details about currency matters:

1. Denominations: Euros are available in coins and banknotes. Coins are available in 1, 2, 5, 10, 20, and 50 cent denominations in addition to 1 and 2 euros. Banknotes are issued in 5, 10, 20, 50, 100, 200, and 500 euro denominations.

2. Currency Exchange: Currency exchange services are available at airports, banks, and exchange offices in major towns. ATMs are widespread and allow you to withdraw euros using your debit or credit card.

3. Credit Cards: Credit and debit cards are widely accepted in hotels, restaurants, and shops. Visa and MasterCard are commonly used, while American Express and Diners Club may be taken in some places.

4. ATMs: ATMs are easily accessible in urban areas and tourist destinations. It's advisable to inform your bank of your travel dates to avoid any issues with card transactions.

5. Tipping: Tipping is a common practice in restaurants, cafes, and for services. While it's not obligatory, rounding up the bill or leaving a small percentage (5-10%) is appreciated.

Language in Corfu

The official language of Corfu, and Greece in general, is Greek. However, due to the island's popularity as a tourist destination, English is widely spoken, especially in tourist areas, hotels, and restaurants. Here are some language-related considerations:

1. Common Greek Phrases

Learning a few basic Greek phrases can enhance your experience and show appreciation for the local culture. Common greetings include "Kalimera" (Good morning), "Kalispera" (Good evening), and "Efharisto" (Thank you).

2. English Proficiency

English is spoken by many locals involved in the tourism industry. In major towns and tourist attractions, you'll find that communication in English is generally smooth.

3. Local Dialects

While Greek is the primary language, some older residents may speak a local Corfiot dialect. However, this is rare among the younger population.

4. Multilingual Signage

Public signs, especially in tourist areas, are often in Greek and English. This makes navigation and understanding important information more accessible for international visitors.

5. Cultural Sensitivity

While English is commonly spoken, making an effort to use basic Greek phrases can be appreciated by locals. It shows respect for the local culture and is often met with a warm reception.

Navigating Corfu with a basic understanding of the local currency and language will provide a more seamless and enjoyable travel experience. Whether exploring historic sites, dining in traditional tavernas, or engaging with locals, these insights will serve you well.

Safety Tips for a Secure Stay in Corfu

Ensuring your safety is paramount while exploring Corfu. Follow these tips to have a secure and worry-free experience on the island:

1. Emergency Numbers

Familiarize yourself with emergency contact numbers, including 112 for general emergencies, 100 for police, 166 for medical assistance, and 199 for the fire department.

2. Travel Insurance

Obtain comprehensive travel insurance covering medical emergencies, trip cancellations, and unforeseen incidents. Confirm that it includes coverage for activities you plan to engage in.

3. Health Precautions

Carry any necessary prescription medications, a basic first aid kit, and essential medical documents. Check if vaccinations or specific health precautions are recommended before traveling.

4. Safe Transportation

Use reputable transportation services, whether taxis, rental cars, or public transportation. Confirm the legitimacy of drivers and vehicles, and buckle up for safety.

5. Awareness of Surroundings

Stay vigilant and know your surroundings, especially in crowded or unfamiliar areas. Keep an eye on your belongings to prevent pickpocketing.

6. Natural Hazards

Be mindful of natural hazards when engaging in outdoor activities like hiking or swimming. Follow safety guidelines, weather conditions, and any warnings local authorities provide.

7. Water Safety

Exercise caution when swimming, especially in areas without lifeguards. Be aware of currents and follow any safety flags or guidelines on beaches.

8. Local Laws and Customs

To guarantee polite behavior, familiarize oneself with the laws and customs of the area. In Greece, smoking is prohibited in indoor public spaces, and it's customary to dress modestly when visiting religious sites.

9. Secure Accommodations

Choose reputable accommodations with secure locks and safety features. Use hotel safes for valuables and keep important documents secure.

10. Sun Protection

Corfu enjoys a sunny climate, so protect yourself from sun exposure. Use sunscreen, wear a hat, and stay hydrated, especially during outdoor activities.

11. Food and Water Safety

Drink bottled or filtered water and eat at respectable restaurants. Be cautious with street food and ensure that meals are prepared and stored hygienically.

12. Cultural Sensitivity

Respect local customs and traditions. Ask for permission before taking photographs, particularly in religious or private spaces.

13. Local Advice

Seek advice from locals or your accommodation hosts regarding safe areas, potential risks, and recommended precautions. They are able to offer insightful advice.

14. Communication

Keep communication devices charged and have local emergency numbers saved. Inform someone trustworthy about your plans if engaging in outdoor or remote activities.

By staying informed, exercising caution, and respecting local customs, you can ensure a safe and enjoyable visit to Corfu. These tips contribute to a positive travel experience while prioritizing your well-being.

Chapter Nine

Crafting Memorable Experiences in Corfu

Corfu offers a tapestry of experiences that linger in your memory. Immerse yourself in the island's charm and create lasting moments with these suggestions:

1. Sunset at Kaiser's Throne

Head to Kaiser's Throne in Pelekas for a breathtaking sunset. The panoramic view of the Ionian Sea, especially during the golden hour, is a mesmerizing experience.

2. Boat Trip to Paxos and Antipaxos

Embark on a boat excursion to the nearby islands of Paxos and Antipaxos. Discover secluded beaches, sea caves, and the turquoise waters of the Ionian Sea.

3. Traditional Corfiot Cuisine

Delight your taste buds with Corfu's culinary treasures. Enjoy a leisurely meal at a traditional taverna, savoring dishes like moussaka, pastitsada, and fresh seafood.

4. Corfu Trail Hike - Angelokastro to Lakones

Hike a section of the Corfu Trail from Angelokastro to Lakones. The scenic route unveils historic sites, picturesque landscapes, and stunning coastline views.

5. Cultural Exploration in Corfu Town

Wander through Corfu Town's UNESCO-listed Old Town. Explore the Esplanade and Liston Promenade, and visit landmarks like the Old and New Fortresses, St. Spyridon Church, and the Archaeological Museum.

6. Relaxation at Canal d'Amour Beach

Visit Canal d'Amour Beach in Sidari, known for its unique sandstone formations. Legend has it that couples who swim through the Canal will get married soon.

7. Achilleion Palace and Gardens

Explore the Achilleion Palace, a neoclassical gem with lush gardens. Admire the panoramic views, statues, and opulent interiors once owned by Empress of Austria Elisabeth of Bavaria.

8. Live Music at Corfu Town's Liston Square

Experience the vibrant atmosphere of Liston Square in the evening. Enjoy live music from local bands, sip coffee or cocktails, and soak in the lively ambiance.

9. Cruise along the Paleokastritsa Caves

Take a boat tour to explore the sea caves around Paleokastritsa. The crystal-clear waters reveal hidden wonders beneath the surface, creating a magical experience.

10. Visit a Traditional Olive Mill

Gain insight into Corfu's olive oil production by visiting a traditional olive mill. Learn about the cultivation process and taste the island's liquid gold.

11. Folklore Museum of Acharavi

Immerse yourself in Corfu's cultural heritage at the Folklore Museum of Acharavi. Discover exhibits showcasing traditional costumes, crafts, and artifacts.

12. Scuba Diving in Kassiopi

Explore Corfu's underwater world by diving in Kassiopi. Dive centers offer experiences for all levels, allowing you to discover the rich marine life and captivating seascapes.

13. Traditional Easter Celebrations

If visiting during Easter, witness Corfu's unique Easter celebrations. The town comes alive with processions, music, and the renowned "Liston egg smashing" tradition.

14. Coffee in a Hidden Courtyard in Corfu Town

Discover hidden courtyards in Corfu Town. Enjoy coffee in these serene spaces, away from the bustling streets, and absorb the local charm.

15. Capture the Essence of Nymphes Waterfall

Visit Nymphes Village to discover the hidden waterfall. Capture the essence of this serene spot surrounded by lush greenery, creating a peaceful and picturesque memory.

These experiences weave together the fabric of Corfu's allure. Whether exploring history, savoring local flavors, or basking in the natural beauty, each moment adds to the tapestry of your unforgettable journey.

Unique Activities for an Unforgettable Corfu Trip

Elevate your Corfu adventure with these distinctive activities, ensuring your trip is nothing short of extraordinary:

1. Olive Harvest Experience

Participate in the olive harvest season (usually in autumn). Engage in the traditional process, from picking olives to pressing them into oil. Some local farms offer hands-on experiences.

2. Corfiot Wine Tasting Tour

Explore Corfu's wineries and vineyards on a wine-tasting tour. Sample indigenous varieties like Robiola and Kakotrygis paired with local cheeses and delicacies.

3. Byzantine Trails Exploration

Venture off the beaten path to discover Byzantine trails that wind through Corfu's scenic landscapes. These ancient paths offer a unique perspective on the island's history and natural beauty.

4. Traditional Greek Cooking Class

Immerse yourself in Corfiot cuisine with a hands-on cooking class. Learn to prepare local dishes like pastitsada, moussaka, or baklava under the guidance of skilled chefs.

5. Donkey Trekking in the Countryside

Embark on a donkey trekking adventure through Corfu's rural Countryside. Traverse olive groves and charming villages while accompanied by these gentle and friendly animals.

6. Birdwatching in Korission Lake

Korission Lake is a haven for birdwatching enthusiasts. Spot diverse bird species in this natural reserve, including flamingos, herons, and various migratory birds.

7. Night Snorkeling in Paleokastritsa

Experience the enchanting world beneath the waves with a night snorkeling excursion in Paleokastritsa. Witness marine life in a different light under the moonlit sea.

8. Corfu's Traditional Pottery Workshops

Unleash your creativity at a traditional pottery workshop. Craft your souvenir under the guidance of skilled artisans, incorporating Corfu's artistic heritage.

9. Sunset Horseback Riding in Acharavi

Take a horseback riding excursion along the beach at Acharavi during the golden hour. Witness a breathtaking sunset while riding along the shoreline.

10. Open-Air Cinema in Corfu Town

Enjoy a movie night with a twist at one of Corfu Town's open-air cinemas. Under the stars, savor cinematic experiences in unique settings.

11. Visit the Monastery of Paleokastritsa by Boat

Access the Monastery of Paleokastritsa by boat for a serene and scenic approach. Explore the monastery grounds and take in panoramic views of the coastline.

12. Bike Tour through Corfu's Villages

Discover the island's hidden gems on a bike tour through traditional villages. Wind through narrow lanes, past olive groves, and absorb the local atmosphere.

13. Greek Mythology Walking Tour

Dive into Greek mythology with a guided walking tour. Explore sites associated with ancient myths and legends, unraveling the island's mythical connections.

14. Painting Workshop in Old Perithia

Unleash your artistic side with a painting workshop in the historic village of Old Perithia. Capture the essence of Corfu's architecture and landscapes on canvas.

15. Stargazing Night in the Countryside

Escape the city lights for a stargazing night in Corfu's Countryside. Experience the magic of the night sky and constellations away from urban glare.

These unique activities promise an unforgettable journey, connecting you with Corfu's essence in distinctive and enriching ways. Each experience adds a layer of depth to your travel narrative.

Recommendations for a Memorable Trip

1. Explore Beyond the Tourist Trail: Venture into lesser-known villages, hidden courtyards, and ancient paths to discover the true essence of Corfu.

2. Engage with Locals: Connect with the warm-hearted locals to gain insights into the island's traditions, stories, and vibrant culture.

3. Culinary Delights: Indulge in Corfu's gastronomic treasures, from traditional tavernas to cooking classes, and savor the flavors that define the island.

4. Nature's Embrace: Whether hiking through olive groves, snorkeling in crystal-clear waters, or horseback riding at sunset, let nature guide you.

5. Cultural Immersion: Immerse yourself in Corfu's rich history by exploring ancient fortresses, Byzantine trails, and local museums.

Recommendations for Crafting a Memorable Corfu Trip

As you prepare for your Corfu adventure, consider these recommendations to ensure a journey filled with lasting memories and enriching experiences:

1. Diverse Exploration

Venture beyond the well-trodden paths. Explore the bustling streets of Corfu Town and the tranquil villages in the island's interior for a comprehensive experience.

2. Local Connections

Engage with locals to discover the heartbeat of Corfu. From chatting with shopkeepers to sharing stories with villagers, these interactions add depth to your understanding of the island's culture.

3. Culinary Odyssey

Delight in Corfu's culinary delights. Savor traditional dishes in local tavernas, attend a cooking class to learn the art of Corfiot cuisine, and indulge in fresh seafood by the sea.

4. Nature's Bounty

Immerse yourself in Corfu's natural beauty. Whether it's hiking through olive groves, swimming in secluded coves, or basking in the serenity of the Countryside, let nature be your guide.

5. Historical Exploration

Uncover Corfu's rich history by visiting iconic landmarks such as the Old and New Fortresses, Achilleion Palace, and the Archaeological

Museum. Consider guided tours for deeper insights.

6. Blend of Old and New

Experience the seamless blend of old and new in Corfu Town. Stroll through the historic Old Town, explore modern cafes on the Liston Promenade, and witness the convergence of tradition and modernity.

7. Attend Local Events

Check for local festivals, events, or cultural celebrations during your visit. Participating in these festivities provides a unique window into Corfu's vibrant traditions.

8. Water Adventures

Embrace Corfu's coastal charm with water activities. Snorkel in crystal-clear waters, take a boat trip to nearby islands, or relax on the island's diverse beaches.

9. Photographic Exploration

Capture the essence of Corfu through photography. From the charming architecture of Corfu Town to the scenic landscapes of the Countryside, document the moments that resonate with you.

10. Flexible Itinerary

Allow for spontaneity in your itinerary. Serendipitous discoveries often lead to the most memorable experiences, whether stumbling upon a hidden gem or engaging in an unplanned adventure.

11. Local Arts and Crafts

Explore Corfu's artisanal side by visiting local workshops and galleries. Acquire handmade souvenirs, from olive wood crafts to traditional ceramics, as mementos of your journey.

12. Relaxation and Reflection

Find moments for relaxation and reflection. Whether sipping coffee in a hidden courtyard, enjoying a tranquil sunset, or simply taking a stroll, allow time for quiet moments.

You'll create a tapestry of experiences embodying the island's essence by weaving these recommendations into your Corfu itinerary. Each recommendation is a thread in your memorable journey through Corfu. Safe travels

Conclusion

As your Corfu adventure approaches, reflect on the tapestry of experiences woven through this enchanting island. From the historic charm of Corfu Town to the tranquil beaches and hidden gems, the journey has been a mosaic of memories.

Corfu's allure lies not only in its sun-kissed landscapes but also in the warmth of its people. The fusion of history, culture, and natural beauty creates a destination that lingers in your heart. Embrace the laid-back rhythm, savor the local flavors, and immerse yourself in the rich tapestry of Corfu's identity.

As the sun sets on your Corfu adventure, let's reflect on the tapestry of experiences that have colored your stay. The island's charm, a fusion of history, nature, and warm hospitality, has left an indelible mark on your travel narrative.

Corfu's landscapes, from the azure coastline to the lush interior, compose a symphony of beauty that resonates with every step. The iconic sights, the hidden corners, and the vibrant colors have painted a picture of an island that captivates the soul.

Corfu's rich history, steeped in mythology and marked by various civilizations, unfolds like a captivating story. Exploring ancient fortresses, Byzantine trails, and traditional villages is a journey through time, connecting you to the island's cultural tapestry.

The culinary journey through Corfu has been a feast for the senses. From traditional tavernas to intimate cooking classes, each meal has celebrated local flavors, offering a taste of the island's gastronomic heritage.

Corfu's true treasure lies in the warmth of its people. Engaging with locals has provided insights into their traditions, stories, and the genuine hospitality that makes every visitor feel like a welcomed guest.

Whether navigating through olive groves, snorkeling in crystal-clear waters, or horseback riding at sunset, you've embraced the island's natural wonders. Corfu's landscapes become a backdrop and an active participant in your journey.

Corfu isn't just a destination; it's a chapter in your travel story. The memories forged here – the laughter, the sunsets, the culinary discoveries – create a mosaic that is uniquely yours. As you bid farewell, carry these moments as souvenirs of a journey well-lived.

In the final chords of your Corfu symphony, may the echoes of this vibrant island linger in your heart, a constant reminder of the beauty that awaits in every exploration. Until the next adventure, may the spirit of Corfu accompany you on your journey. Safe travels!

In conclusion, Corfu transcends the realm of a mere travel destination; it becomes a cherished chapter in your journey. As you bid farewell to this Ionian gem, carry with you the memories of sunsets, laughter, and the timeless beauty of Corfu. Until the next adventure, let the spirit of this island linger as a beacon of wanderlust. Safe travels!

Printed in Great Britain
by Amazon